Praise for *Saved Under My Skirt*...

"The Saved Under My Skirt Conference was phenomenal! Keisha discussed relationship wisdom, abstaining from sexual temptation, and shared testimonies explaining how to walk this journey. In the presence of the Holy Spirit, her transparency about struggles and victories helped attendees break free of soul ties. I will never be the same. I'm telling other young ladies about it so they can also experience transformation."
— Trushana Martin

"*Saved Under My Skirt* is a woman's must-have, must-read guide of biblical principles and practical tools to help you experience personal and relational fulfillment."
— Valerie J. Lewis Coleman, author of the bestselling novel, *The Forbidden Secrets of the Goody Box*

"*Saved Under My Skirt* expands far beyond a good idea into a God-ordained assignment! This subject is eye-catching, thought-provoking, and life-changing. Its acronym, S.U.M.S., sums up the truth!"
— Bev Duffey-Martin, Ph.D.

"In a world filled with brokenness, Keisha R. Mitchell helps women experience wholeness and restore integrity. She guides you to understand that you can be healed, complete, and fulfilled in Christ."
— Arto Woodley, Ed.D.

"What an amazing event! The Saved Under My Skirt Conference was a safe place for transparency, healing, and deliverance from brokenness, hurt, and despair. God ignited my spark and my life is forever changed!"
— Lisa Fletcher

"Timely and needed, the Saved Under My Skirt Conference was an amazing experience. For too long, believers have compromised their faith for temporary pleasure. Keisha, because of your boldness and anointing, women were encouraged and set free."
— Ashley McGuire

"The Saved Under My Skirt Conference addressed pre-marital sex and celibacy by explaining what God requires and why. Hearts opened as Keisha shared personal relationship experiences and what God revealed to her regarding sexual purity and integrity."
— LaJuana Henderson

Saved Under My Skirt
Restoring Sexual Integrity

Keisha R. Mitchell

Published by

Royal Keys Publishing
Dayton, OH

Published by
Royal Keys Publishing
Dayton, OH
Copyright © 2022 by Keisha R. Mitchell

ISBN-13: 979-8-9872348-0-8
Library of Congress Control Number: 2022921693

Front cover image designed by Roxane Smith of RNS Marketing Solutions.
Proofread by Sharahnne Gibbons of Something in Comma.

Printed in the United States of America

Dedication

This book is dedicated to the Mitchell girls, my precious daughters, Hannah, and twins, Alexandria and Alexia.

And to my Lord and Savior, Jesus Christ, for His patience, love, and endless mercies toward me.

"To choose celibacy, Jesus must really be precious to you. You only give up something awesome for something even better."

Rachel Gibson

Acknowledgments

First, I thank God for giving me the vision of *Saved Under My Skirt, Restoring Sexual Integrity.* He entrusted me to develop the vision and carry it out. He called and I answered with workshops and conferences for women who desire to please Him by living a life of celibacy. Now, God has used me to write this book, and I am thankful and anticipating much more to come. Thank you, Lord.

I would not be who I am without my parents, Willie Mitchell and Margie Mitchell Shears. The strength of my father and the tenderness of my mother created a gentle giant within me, who digs and grinds with grace and humility. Mom and Dad, thank you for raising me to serve the Lord and treat people with kindness.

To my daughters, Hannah, Alexandria, and Alexia, my biggest supporters and cheerleaders. You push me to be better. I strive to excel to inspire you to reach for the stars with confidence and accomplish more than I ever dreamed of achieving. May God direct your steps and keep you wherever your journeys take you.

To Roxane Smith of RNS Marketing Solutions, thank you for designing my logo and breathing life into my vision. You captured my vision and brought it alive.

Thank you, Maranatha Worship Centre for hosting the first *Saved Under My Skirt* Workshop.

A big thank you to my proofreader, Sharahnne Gibbons of Something in Comma, and my publishing mentor, Valerie J. Lewis Coleman of Pen of the Writer.

Lastly, I acknowledge my past mistakes, failed relationships, and struggles. My experiences made me stronger, wiser, and a testament of God's everlasting love and never-ending mercy. *Saved Under My Skirt* was birthed from my past and will change lives in future generations by the power of God.

Table of Contents

Introduction

After nineteen years of marriage, divorce disrupted my life. Shattered, empty, and lacking faith, I ran from God like a track star trying to win an Olympic gold medal.

I never expected my marriage to fail. Who does? Divorce is difficult enough; however, compounded with marriage to a pastor, my life was on public display for the church to judge. Gossip spread across the country like an uncontrollable wildfire. Fabricated tales and concocted stories fanned the flames of my pain, bitterness, and resentment. The betrayal was unbearable as the spreaders of lies were those who claimed to love God…and me.

I did not want anything to do with God or His people. Treachery of friends and ministry partners soured my spirit and hardened my heart. I turned away from God and the call on my life. I befriended ungodly people and dated worldly men. I intentionally avoided men who were churchgoers. If he had any resemblance to a church boy, I ignored him and blocked his number. Since the good guy didn't work for me, my interest shifted to gold teeth, French braids, and wife beaters…a roughneck. I fornicated knowing it was wrong and grievous to the Lord.

My bad choices continued until God revealed to me the ungodly soul ties I had created. He removed the blindfolds shaped from deep hurt and allowed me to see into the spiritual realm. I dreamt of an ex-boyfriend walking into my bedroom. He crawled under the sheets from the foot of the bed and laid next to me. He rubbed his body against mine until we were stuck together as one. Startled awake, I patted the bed feeling for him, and then sat up to look for him. I just knew he was there.

I asked the Lord, "What was that?"

The Lord replied, "A soul tie."

My soul was intertwined with a man who was not my husband. I knew I had to change if I wanted to be free. I fasted for thirty days, eating only fruits, vegetables, and food grown from the earth. I drank water, prayed, and read the Bible every day. I separated myself from anyone and anything that could distract me from hearing God. Within twenty-one days of my consecration and rededication, God destroyed the soul tie and delivered me from sexual immorality. The weight was lifted. I was filled with His peace and joy. I had been set free.

I have been celibate for four-and-a-half years. I will continue this walk of abstinence until I am married to the man God has ordained for me. I wrote this book as a devotion and prayer journal because I desire for you to be free of sexual sin as God freed me. I feel like the great Harriet Tubman, who once free, returned to free others.

Are you tired of being a sex toy for men who only use you for sexual pleasure? Do you believe you are worth more than a booty call? Are you ready to overcome sexual sin that leaves you emotionally drained and void of dignity? If you answered "Yes" to any of these questions, then *Saved Under My Skirt: Restoring Sexual Integrity* is for you.

This twenty-one-day faith-based devotion and prayer journal was written to help you know your value and understand just how precious you are to God. This book will help you recognize the importance of sexual purity and God's perspective on sex outside of marriage. I created it to help restore sexual integrity and self-worth, and release you from giving yourself to a man who is not your husband. As you meditate on the Word and dive into the assignments, you will be empowered to stop ungodly sexual relations.

This book gives you spiritual tools that will help you withstand the temptations of sexual promiscuity, including prayers, devotions, and fasting* strategies to break the chains of bondage and bring forth your transformation. After each reading, journal your thoughts, feelings, and what the Lord speaks to you. *Saved Under My Skirt* will encourage, edify, and challenge you to rise above sexual sin so you, too, can be set apart for God's use.

Now is the time to shift your thoughts, words, and actions toward a new life.

Keisha R. Mitchell

* Consult with a medical professional before starting any fast.

"To walk a life of celibacy is a choice. A choice that yields peace, bountiful blessings, and eternal life."

Keisha R. Mitchell

Day 1

My Body, His Temple

*Know ye not that your body is the temple of
the Holy Ghost which is in you, which ye
have of God, and ye are not your own?*
—1 Corinthians 6:19

Fast: Refrain from all social media for 24 hours.

The first thing you must fully understand and hold close to your heart is that your body belongs to Christ. He bought you, and it was a costly purchase paid by the blood of Jesus Christ. He purchased you with the sole purpose to live in you. You are His holy temple in which He desires to dwell. You belong to Him and you are not your own.

When you are tempted by the lust of your flesh and the desires of your old nature to give your body to a man that is not your husband, remember God's love for you is boundless, so much so, that He gave the life of His Son so He could call you His beloved daughter. The love God has for you is unrivaled and the investment He made to secure your soul is invaluable, and neither should be compromised for five minutes of temporal pleasure.

Today's Prayer:

Dear Heavenly Father, today, and always, I present my body to You as a living sacrifice, holy and acceptable to You, which is my reasonable service. I cancel every diabolical plot the enemy has schemed to have me engaged in sexual immorality with my body and mind. My body belongs to You, and I want You to dwell fully in me. Today is the beginning of a new journey in which I will be intentional in serving You. Amen.

Day 2

Serve God as Your Husband

> *For thy Maker is thine husband; the Lord of hosts is His name; and thy Redeemer the Holy One of Israel; The God of the whole earth shall he be called.*
> — Isaiah 54:5

Fast: Eliminate all breads from your diet for 24 hours.

Until God brings your husband in your life, serve the Lord as if He were your husband. The time and attention, and all the effort you would give to your husband to have a fruitful and fulfilling marriage, give it to God. While you wait on your Boaz, dedicate your time to doing the work of the ministry. Seek God's face, indulge in His Word, and devote a special time for worship, giving God all that you desire to give your coming husband.

While you wait for the man of your dreams to manifest in your reality, tend to God's business. When he shows up, remember your God and keep yourself sanctified. Once the man you have been praying for arrives, please understand sex will not make him stay. Keep yourself honorable before God. Respect yourself, and if he is the real one and not a counterfeit, he will respect you, too, and wait for sex until you both say, "I do."

Today's Prayer:

Dear Heavenly Father, I thank You for Your love for me, and for keeping me pure and consecrated until You see fit for me to be wed with whom You have predestined for me. Father God, I will continue to serve You with my entire being as You align me with Your purpose and plan. Be with me and lead me that I may be found in Your perfect will. Amen.

Keisha R. Mitchell

Day 3

Empty Out

Therefore also now, saith the Lord, turn ye even to me with all your heart, and with fasting, and with weeping, and with mourning.
—Joel 2:12

Fast: Eliminate meats from your diet for 24 hours.

Fasting is an essential part of your walk with God. It is a way to humble yourself in the sight of the Lord. When you fast, you deny yourself food and the pleasures of this life. You become empty to make space and create the capacity to receive and hold what God has to deposit in you. If your appetite is satisfied and you are full of carnality, you have no capacity for God to fill you.

Fasting keeps you empty and open for God to deposit His power, His Word, and His glory in you. You cannot host both God and carnality. You have to clean out your house for the Lord to dwell. The Lord deposits a Word in your heart, but you cannot contain it, because you have no space. The Lord needs you empty. Live a fasted life, so you can clearly hear his voice and have room to receive all He wants to give you.

Become an empty vessel. Turn down your plate and turn your heart fully to God. Cry out to the Lord and evict everything in your life that is a distraction and a hindrance from you drawing closer to God.

Today's Prayer:

Dear Heavenly Father, I empty myself, so You can fully dwell in me. Fill my cup, Lord, so that it overflows. I will commit to a fasted life and deny worldly pleasures. Whatever occupies space in me that prevents You from depositing in me, I let go of it now. Amen.

_____

_____

_____

_____

_____

_____

_____

_____

_____

_____

_____

_____

_____

_____

_____

_____

_____

_____

_____

_____

Keisha R. Mitchell

"To gain victory over the flesh was the purpose of fasting and celibacy, which denied the pleasures of this world for the sake of reward in the next."

Barbara Tuchman

Day 4

Severing Soul Ties

*"What? Know ye not that he which is joined
to an harlot is one body? for two, saith he,
shall be one flesh."*
—1 Corinthians 6:16

Fast: Refrain from watching television for 24 hours.

Dear Sister, when you sexually join yourself with a man who is not your husband, a soul tie is created. Two souls, your and his, are tied together as one. You are linked emotionally and have developed the one-flesh principle, which God designed for a husband and wife. Sex is to be reserved for your husband, if not, unholy soul ties are bred.

When you try to leave these ungodly relationships, it is grievous. It is painfully hard to sever a soul tie because every time you try to leave, you feel the pain of the tearing away of the souls. Bearing this agony is grueling, so you often find yourself back in a relationship that is contrary to the will of God for your life.

Destroying a soul tie is difficult; however, by the power of God, it can be conquered. Dive into God's presence and allow Him to shred the cords of entanglement. Whom the Son sets free is free indeed.

Today's Prayer:

Dear Heavenly Father, I ask that You annihilate every soul tie and every unfruitful connection that I allowed to take root in my life. I pray that You bestow grace and mercy unto me as I cut off relationships that are not part of my destiny. I declare every soul tie has been crucified at the cross and no longer has power over me. Amen.

Keisha R. Mitchell

Day 5

Keep Your Pearls

Give not that which is holy unto the dogs, neither cast ye your pearls before swine, lest they trample them under their feet, and turn again and rend you.
— Matthew 7:6

Fast: Refrain from eating sweets and any food containing sugar for 24 hours.

God calls you a royal priesthood and a holy nation. He admonishes you to be holy as He is holy. You are holy because God has called you holy. The Lord says, don't give what is holy unto the dogs.

My dear sister, you are a treasure and a precious gem in the eyes of the Lord. Do not give yourself to the dogs who only want your bones. You are worth more than a one-night stand. You are worth more than a "booty call." You are a pearl; beautiful, rare, and unique. You are made in the likeness of God and are worth more than being a doggie treat.

The gifts and calling God deposited in you are valuable, and the man God has for you will recognize that value and cherish you. The spouse God has ordained for you will protect your value and add to it. He will not disrespect or dishonor you, but He will be your lifelong partner and grow in holiness with you.

Today's Prayer:

Dear Heavenly Father, help me to realize my value. Help me to know, with certainty, that I am holy because You have called me holy. This day, I commit to walking in Your truth about me, knowing that I am valuable. I will protect my holiness and guard my worth along with all You have placed in me from the dogs and the swine. And Lord, help me to recognize the dogs when they come into my presence. Amen.

Keisha R. Mitchell

"When you really see how much God loves you, there's no greater love than that. I had to match the amount of love He has for me, which is the reason why I decided to take a vow of celibacy."

Jessica White

Day 6

Harvest Time is Coming

And let us not be weary in well doing: for in due season we shall reap, if we faint not.
—Galatians 6:9

Fast: Drink only water with meals and throughout the day for 24 hours.

As you continue this journey striving to please God with your body, be encouraged. The sacrifices you make to honor the Lord are received as a sweet-smelling fragrance. Every date you declined and each sexual advance you resisted for the sake of Christ, has been recorded in heaven. Temptation is ever present, yet you continue to overcome and persevere through every trial and test.

Reaping Season is coming. Continue to deny yourself of fleshly pleasure to glorify God in your body. Keep your temple clean and free of sin, so the Holy Spirit can fully fill you. You may get tired of living upright while watching others around you live abominably, but do not stop standing for godliness. You will reap a bountiful harvest in due season.

Today's Prayer:

Dear Heavenly Father, I pray for Your strength to sustain me while I await my harvest. Soak me in Your grace so that when I get weary, I will not fold. I need Your power to carry me through my low moments. When I feel exhausted, breathe on me, dear Lord. Blow Your breath of life on my soul. Amen.

Keisha R. Mitchell

Day 7

Walking in Agreement

Can two walk together, except they be agreed?
— Amos 3:3

Fast: Choose your own fast.

Walking in harmony and unity is essential for a peaceable life with your partner. There are many issues in life in which individuals have different viewpoints and sentiments. From saving money to rearing children, from religion to physical intimacy, relationships struggle and often fail, because people do not walk in agreement.

Having companionship with a man who understands your longing to please God with your body is crucial to your celibacy journey. Not only should he understand, but also walk in agreement with you. You are endeavoring to live a chastened life, fleeing fornication and sexual immorality. You cannot afford to have a boyfriend who pressures you into sexual interaction. The two of you have to be in accord and agree to engage in activities that bring spiritual fulfillment and glory to God. It is better to be alone than to be attached to someone who is not in sync with your mission to please your Father in Heaven.

Today's Prayer:

Dear Heavenly Father, I ask that You give me the courage to release anyone in my life who does not line up with my values and personal beliefs. I ask that You bring the right man, and people, in my circle who desire to please You with their mind, body, and soul as I do. Please help me identify those who pretend to be like-minded and have ill intentions. Please sharpen my spiritual gifts that I might discern correctly. Amen.

"Celibacy is not just a matter of not having sex. It is a way of admiring a person for their humanity, maybe even their beauty."

Timothy Radcliffe

Day 8

Run for the Exit

There hath no temptation taken you such as is common to man: but God is faithful, who will not suffer you to be tempted above that ye are able; but will with the temptation also make a way to escape, that ye may be able to bear it.
—1 Corinthians 10:13

Fast: Only eat fresh fruits and vegetables for 24 hours.

There will be times when you will be tempted, even as Jesus was tempted in the Garden of Gethsemane. Temptation will come when you least expect it and often at a point in time when you are weak. When you are being enticed, and find yourself in compromising situations, know that God has already prepared a way of escape.

The enemy's primary goal is to draw you away from God, and he lures you by the lust of your flesh. The enemy will tempt you with the hope that you will fall into his trap, which leads to sin and destruction. But, be strong in the Lord and the power of His might. Put on the full armor of God that you may be able to stand against the enemy, and while you stand, find the escape exit God has already provided for you.

Today's Prayer:

Dear Heavenly Father, I pray, today, for Your plan of escape to be made clear to me when I am tempted. Help me not to fall to temptations the enemy has set before me. Give me the power to say no to the things my flesh desires, which displease you. When I am weak, be my strength. When I feel like giving up and giving in, carry me. When I fall, catch me. Amen.

Keisha R. Mitchell

Day 9

Fire and Desire

I say therefore to the unmarried and the widows, it is good for them if they abide even as I. But if they cannot contain, let them marry: for it is better to marry than to burn.
—1 Corinthians 7:8-9

Fast: Refrain from all social activities for 24 hours.

As a single woman, you can freely do the work of the ministry without having to balance your time with the needs of a husband. You have the liberty to serve at your church and in your community while bypassing the responsibilities a wife has to her spouse. The opportunities to pursue your dreams and the call of God on your life are greater when you have fewer people entitled to your time and attention.

However, on the flip side, you sometimes feel alone and yearn for companionship and intimacy. The desire to have someone hold you at night and kiss you when you open your eyes in the morning is clashing with your desire to abstain from sexual sin. Wanting to please God and please self is a perpetual battle you will have to fight. Rather than giving in to fornication, be honest with God and ask Him to send you your husband for your soul's sake, because He said, "for it is better to marry than to burn."

Today's Prayer:

Heavenly Father, I need You. My heart longs to make You proud, and at the same time, it longs to have companionship and the love of a husband. Some days it is a face-off. I will continue to wait on You, trust in Your timing, and have faith that You will watch over my soul and secure my future. Amen.

Day 10

God is Bigger

Ye are of God, little children, and have overcome them: because greater is he that is in you, than he that is in the world.
—1 John 4:4

Fast: Refrain from eating, drinking water only from the time you awake until 6:00 p.m.

Whatever challenges you may encounter — depression, anxiety, divorce, unexpected pregnancy, or finances — please know without a doubt that God is greater. He is bigger than any problem you are up against. He is the creator of the universe. He flung the stars and the moon into the sky and created night and day. Surely, He can handle any situation you are facing.

Be encouraged today. God is taking care of everything that concerns you. He has not forgotten about you, and He hears your heart's cry. He is great, and His greatness is inside of you. Walk in the authority and boldness of Him that is within and speak peace and proclaim victory over every predicament. You are an overcomer. You will triumph over the troubles in this world.

Today's Prayer:

Dear Heavenly Father, I ask You for nothing today. I just want to thank You for being great in me. I thank You for calling me Your child and giving me Your power to overcome whatever problems I face. Thank You for loving me and never leaving me. Thank You for Your unceasing love and for giving me salvation and eternal life. I will forever praise You and magnify Your matchless name. Amen.

Day 11

Tame the Tongue

Death and life are in the power of the tongue: And they that love it shall eat the fruit thereof.
—Proverbs 18:21

Fast: Refrain from all social media for 24 hours.

The words you speak have so much power. Your words can either speak life or your words can speak death. This is why the bible instructs you to not confess anything negative that is in your mind, but rather speak life to every situation. God spoke the entire world into existence, and you as a child of God, have that same power to make your words come alive.

Whatever it is that you desire, speak it into the atmosphere. Declare the year you will be married. Proclaim the family you wish to create. Speak it into existence. The enemy would love for you to keep your mouth shut because he knows the power that you possess and the power of the spoken words that you utter.

Open your mouth and decree and declare the promises of God.

Today's Prayer:

Dear Heavenly Father, I pray that You increase my faith and help me realize the power my words possess. Help me not to be ashamed or think it is foolish to speak those things that are not as though they were. Give me the assurance of what my words can create as You bring forth the manifestation when I speak. Thank You in advance. Amen.

Day 12

Reservation for Two

Marriage is honorable among all, and the bed undefiled; but fornicators and adulterers God will judge.
—Hebrews 13:4

Fast: Refrain from eating, drinking water only from 6:00 p.m. until you wake the next morning.

The only place sexual intimacy should be experienced is in the bed of the married. God designed sexual activity for a husband and his wife. There are no limitations, and nothing is prohibited between a consenting married couple. There should be no kind of sex outside of marriage, including pre-marital, extra-marital, or homosexual activity. Single individuals sometimes find themselves practicing sexual acts as if they were legally wed, and God is not pleased.

Fornication and adultery come with a penalty. Judgment is the "reward" when you engage in sexual sin. A five-minute sexual act could have you tangled up in consequences for the next ten years or more. Before you chose to engage in sexual activity and get caught up, count up the cost. And let's be clear, sexual activity is more than just intercourse, it includes oral sex as well.

Today's Prayer:

Dear Heavenly Father, I repent of any and all sexual activities I have engaged in, which I know displeases You. Forgive me, Dear Lord, of all the impure thoughts I have that perpetuate the desire to engage in sexual acts. Recondition my mind, oh God, that my thoughts may please You and my body will follow. Have mercy on me. Amen.

"We delight in the beauty of the butterfly but rarely admit the changes it has gone through to achieve that beauty."

Maya Angelou

Day 13

For Your Soul's Sake

For this is the will of God, even your sanctification, that ye shall abstain from fornication.
—1 Thessalonians 4:3

Fast: Refrain from sweets and any food that contains sugar for 24 hours.

God desires for you to be sanctified and set apart for special use for Him. Being sanctified takes deliberate action on your part. Making Godly choices and resisting sexual immorality should be purposeful and at the forefront of your mind.

Why does God will for you to be sanctified? Why does He tell you to abstain from fornication specifically? There are consequences to fornication, and God does not want you to suffer those consequences. Fornication yields emotional damage, health risk through sexually transmitted diseases, and most significantly, separation from God. The Lord wants to protect you from these outcomes, so he implores you to be sanctified.

Fornication will also have you feeling empty, scattered, and void of self-worth. Partly because you have given yourself away to men who are not your husband, and now you are missing pieces of yourself.

Today's Prayer:

Dear Heavenly Father, I pray for a spirit of holiness and purity to overtake me. I release my will and I accept Your will for me. Fornication and sexual immorality have no place in my life. Fill me up, so there is no room for anything that is not like You. My ultimate goal is to please You and to live holy in Your sight. Amen.

Keisha R. Mitchell

"When you embrace celibacy, other elements of the relationship have to come forth. There isn't an opportunity for you to be blinded by your sexual desires; however, there is an opportunity to see things more clearly."

Edwina Findley

Day 14

WAP

I beseech you therefore, brethren, by the mercies of God, that ye present your bodies a living sacrifice, holy, acceptable unto God, which is your reasonable service. And be not conformed to this world: but be ye transformed by the renewing of your mind, that ye may prove what is that good, and acceptable, and perfect, will of God.
— Romans 12:1-2

Fast: Eat only fresh vegetables for 24 hours.

As a woman of God, you portray the attributes of Christ. The fruits of the spirit radiate from you. You are peculiar. You shine bright and stand out amongst those who are not in fellowship with God. Though you live in this world, you do not conform to the things of this world.

The world would have you living contrary to the things of God. From secular music to television programming, believers are flooded with ungodly songs, commercials, and videos. The most disturbing and direct attack against sexual integrity is the song "WAP," Wet A** P***y, by two female rap artists. The song suggests that sex is what gets you a man as well as makes a man marry you. The devil is a lie!

It shall be proclaimed that "WAP" stands for Women Abstaining Promiscuity. Take a stand against the spirit of the world and raise the standard for sexual integrity for young ladies to follow. The world does not set the standard; the body of Christ does.

Today's Prayer:

Dear Heavenly Father, help me to stand tall and firm against the spirit of the world by the power of Your holy spirit. Help me to be transformed daily by renewing my mind with Your Word. Strengthen me that I will not conform to the things of this world. I will be led by Your Word and will not follow. Amen.

Keisha R. Mitchell

Day 15

The Pig's Playpen

Wherefore come out from among them, and be ye separate, saith the Lord, and touch not the unclean thing; and I will receive you.
—2 Corinthians 6:17

Fast: Choose your own fast.

Separate yourself from the works of darkness. Detach yourself from any connections to what God says is unclean. Shut the door to all impure spirits as they lie in wait to have a foothold in your life.

Pornography is a gateway for filthy spirits to enter through. You may not engage in sexual acts; however, pornography fuels lust, fornication, adultery, and homosexuality. Pornography glorifies sexual immorality while God requires sexual purity.

What you allow to come through your eye gate will seep into your mind and ultimately into your heart; and then turns into an act. Pornography imbeds graphic images in your mind and intensifies sexual tension. Pornography is unclean, and God does not want you to have any involvement with what is not clean. His bride is to be pure without spot or wrinkle.

Today's Prayer:

Dear Heavenly Father, I pray for Your delivering power to liberate me from any unclean spirit I have allowed to attach itself to my life. I pray for Your release of guilt and embarrassment for entertaining what You have called polluted. I rebuke and bind lying tormenting spirits that invade my mind. I am Yours and You are mine, and nothing can separate me from Your unfailing love. Amen.

Keisha R. Mitchell

Day 16

What's Your Price Tag?

For ye are bought with a price; therefore glorify God in your body, and your spirit, which are God's.
—1 Corinthians 6:20

Fast: For the first eight hours upon waking, only consume liquids.

God's price for you was the sacrificial offering of His son, Jesus Christ. The love God has for you is immeasurable. God loves you so much that He gave His best to have you. The bridegroom gave a first-class gift for His bride, the church.

If a man wants to be with you, he will take the necessary steps to have you. Whatever he has to do to secure you as his own, he will do. There is no sacrifice too great for true love. If he is truly devoted to you, he will buy you a ring, propose to you, and make you his wife. Without engaging in premarital sex.

Insist on being courted and pursued before committing to a relationship. Require a man to exemplify his love while he labors for yours. As God gave His best for His bride, a man should give his best for his as well.

Today's Prayer:

Dear Heavenly Father, thank You for being an example and displaying unconditional love for Your bride, the church. Help me to wait on the right man who knows how to love like You. Help me to receive true love and know that I am worthy to be loved as You love the church and gave Your very best. Amen.

Keisha R. Mitchell

Day 17

The Virtue Within

*Who can find a virtuous woman? For her
price is above rubies.*
— Proverbs 31:10

Fast: Refrain from eating, drinking water only from
the time you awake until 4:00 p.m.

One of the most beautiful qualities in a woman is a quiet spirit. A calm nature that soothes the soul. A woman can wear all the make-up Mary Kay invented with hair extensions to her waist, and still will not emanate true beauty. Beauty does not come from outward adornments such as false eyelashes, Rolex watches, Channel purses, and Gucci clothes. True beauty comes from within. It is not flamboyant and boisterous, but modest and peaceful.

A virtuous woman is not found within circles of gossipers or amongst those who create division. She is found taking care of her home and affairs and caring for her children. She is disciplined and diligent, trustworthy, and wise. Her value is priceless, and her strength is relentless. Her husband calls her blessed.

You are a virtuous woman. Unlock the virtue that is contained inside of you. Stroll in the beauty that comes from within. You shall be called blessed.

Today's Prayer:

Dear Heavenly Father, I thank You for Your quiet and gentle spirit that rests within me. Help me to release my virtue from within. Remind me daily my true beauty is not in my outward appearance, but within my soul. Help me to operate in my true value and worth, which is more prized than rubies. Amen.

Keisha R. Mitchell

_____

_____

_____

_____

_____

_____

_____

_____

_____

_____

_____

_____

_____

_____

_____

_____

_____

_____

_____

_____

_____

_____

Day 18

Bond in Unity

Be ye not unequally yoked together with unbelievers: for what fellowship hath righteousness with unrighteousness? and what communion hath light with darkness?
—2 Corinthians 6:14

Fast: Refrain from watching television for 24 hours.

It is important to be coupled with a partner of a like mind and spirit as you. How can you be joined with someone who does not believe as you do? What do you have in common? Oil and water do not mix. You see dreams and visions while your partner is spiritually blind. You are seeking the kingdom of God, and he wants to go to the nightclub.

Being a believer and pairing with an unbeliever, directly opposes God's instructions. Coupling with the wicked will hinder your spiritual growth, create internal strife, and disrupt your peace. You will find yourself fighting battles you would have never had if you just waited for your promise. You are the salt of the earth and the light of this world. Why would you willingly be bound with darkness? Do not settle for less than what God wants you to have, which is a partner who walks in righteousness.

Today's Prayer:

Dear Heavenly Father, I will patiently wait for You to deliver Your promise to me. I will be careful not to interfere with the work You are doing on my behalf. Help me, dear Lord, not to get involved with anyone in any way in which You have not intended. I ask that You allow my light to shine bright so that darkness will have to flee. Amen.

Keisha R. Mitchell

Day 19

Where are the Mourning Women?

Thus saith the Lord of hosts, "Consider ye, and call for the mourning women, that they may come; and send for cunning women, that they may come."
— Jeremiah 9:17

Fast: Eliminate all breads from your diet for 24 hours.

This is a clarion call for the mourning women. It is time for the mighty women of God to pray and intercede for their nation against sexual perversion. Cry loud and spare not, for the coming of the Lord is near.

Develop a strong prayer life. Learn to war in the spirit and skillfully pray against the enemy's plots to disengage the kingdom of God. Rebuke and bind the works of darkness and cancel every assignment the enemy has on marriages, pastors, the youth, and the governments.

Teach your daughters to pray, and to mourn for lost souls, those in despair and facing identity crisis. Start up a prayer group and pray with your sisters in Christ and their daughters to bind principalities and wickedness in high places that fight against God's plan on the earth. Pray without ceasing.

Today's Prayer:

Dear Heavenly Father, strengthen my prayer life and help me to pray without ceasing. Increase my spiritual awareness that I may be able to rightly discern and identify the spirits I need to pray against. Open up my spiritual understanding and my spiritual sight. Teach me to be an intercessor and war on the behalf of my family, my church, my community, and my nation. Amen.

Day 20

Willful Worship

And, behold, a woman in the city, which was a sinner, when she knew that Jesus sat at meat in the Pharisee's house, brought an alabaster box ointment, and stood at his feet behind him weeping, and began to wash his feet with tears, and did wiped them with the hairs of her head, and kissed his feet, and anointed them with ointment.
—Luke 7:37-38

Fast: Refrain from eating food, drinking water only from the time you awake until 7:00 p.m.

Mary, the sinful woman in the city, humbled herself and gave Jesus her best worship. She kissed His feet and anointed Him with her most expensive oil. Mary loved Jesus so much that she honored Him with her most valuable possession. Her display of worship to Him was so pure and deliberate others were offended and found fault because she was considered a sinner. She extolled Jesus anyway.

What is stopping you from giving God your best worship? What past sin has paralyzed you, making you feel unworthy to worship God? Go to God and sit at His feet and worship. He loves you and calls you the apple of His eye. When you pour yourself out to Him, He will in return pour His loving kindness unto you, bind up your wounds, and heal all the brokenness in your life.

You were created to worship God. "The true worshippers shall worship the Father in spirit and in truth, for the Father seeks such to worship Him." Worship God, not just with your lips, but with your life.

Today's Prayer:

Dear Heavenly Father, I love You with everything within me. I am nothing without You, and everything I am is because of You. I live and move, because of You. I worship You today with my entire being. I exalt and magnify Your name. You are the air I breathe. You are my Rock. You are the great I Am. You are my all in all. You are everything I need, and I will never stop praising and worshiping Your name. Amen.

Keisha R. Mitchell

"Sexual intercourse is a gift that says, 'Do not open until marriage.' If you've already unwrapped it, wrap it up again!"

Molly Kelly

Day 21

Restoration and Redemption

And Joshua the son of Nun sent out of Shittim two men to spy secretly, saying, "Go view the land, even Jericho." And they went, and come into an harlot's house, named Rahab, and lodged there.
—Joshua 2:1

Fast: Consume only liquids for 24 hours.

Regardless of your past and all the sins you have committed; God will still use you. Just because you have had sexual involvement with someone you were not married to or even with someone else's husband, God will forgive you and clean you up for His use. You possibly could have sold your body for financial gain; however, be encouraged today, God still has use for you.

Rahab was a renowned prostitute in the city of Jericho and God used her mightily. Rahab, a harlot, hid spies sent by Joshua in her home and helped the Israelites in capturing Jericho. God not only used her, but He also saved her and her family's lives from destruction. She and her family were spared because she did as the men of God instructed and hung a scarlet cord from her window when the Israelites invaded the city.

The blood of Jesus covers all your faults and protects you from devastation. There is nothing that cannot be covered under the blood of Christ. Be obedient to the instructions of God. His Word will lead you and bring deliverance. Remember, and never forget, He has a need for you to do His work, and your shortcomings cannot negate the assignment God has on your life.

Today's Prayer:

Dear Heavenly Father, I thank You for Your Son, Jesus Christ, who died on the cross for my sins. I thank You for His blood that blots out all my transgressions. Today, I totally surrender my life to You and proclaim You Lord over my life. I will not allow my past mistakes to hinder me from being used by You. I put my past under the blood, and I put my life in Your hands. Amen.

Keisha R. Mitchell

About Keisha R. Mitchell

For more than twenty-five years, Keisha R. Mitchell has inspired and empowered women. She guides them to redemption by helping them discover their God-given gifts, restoring confidence, and modeling self-worth.

She founded Saved Under My Skirt, LLC to host workshops and conferences for single women who choose celibacy as they await their king of God's choosing. Her mandate is to tear down the works of sexual immorality and restore sexual integrity.

With three daughters watching closely, Keisha models the wholesome lifestyle she wants for all women.

For speaking engagements, workshops, and bulk book purchases of *Saved Under My Skirt*, contact Keisha at savedundermyskirt@gmail.com or visit KeishaRMitchell.com.